IMAGES
of America

CONNECTICUT HURRICANES DRUM & BUGLE CORPS

This slightly tattered treasure is the applique that was proudly displayed on the back of the Connecticut Hurricanes corps jacket around 1955. It is made of navy blue felt, trimmed in white, with white and blue lettering. (Courtesy of James Duplese and the Hurricane archives.)

On the Cover: This photograph from 1939 captures the John H. Collins Post Fife, Drum & Bugle Corps standing proud and erect as they pause during the Derby/Shelton Memorial Day parade. The drum corps is shown crossing the bridge over the Housatonic River as they leave Shelton to enter their hometown of Derby, Connecticut. (Courtesy of the Hurricane archives.)

IMAGES
of America

CONNECTICUT HURRICANES DRUM & BUGLE CORPS

John M. Fisher

ARCADIA
PUBLISHING

ISBN 978-1-4671-0388-6

Published by Arcadia Publishing
Charleston, South Carolina

Printed in the United States of America

Library of Congress Control Number: 2019932497

For all general information, please contact Arcadia Publishing:
Telephone 843-853-2070
Fax 843-853-0044
E-mail sales@arcadiapublishing.com
For customer service and orders:
Toll-Free 1-888-313-2665

Visit us on the Internet at www.arcadiapublishing.com

This book is dedicated to all members of the Connecticut Hurricanes, past, present, and future, as well as to the many friends, family, and communities across the state of Connecticut that have supported and embraced the Hurricanes for nearly nine decades.

Contents

ACKNOWLEDGMENTS

The inspiration for this book derives from my many years of association with the Hurricanes and all of the memories that are refreshed by the countless people I have come to know. Special thanks to Gary Ferris, who provided the impetus and encouragement for me to tackle this project. My appreciation also to Pat Chagnon, Chris Maher, and Lawrence Eckert, drum corps photographers all, as well as Steve Vickers, publisher of *Drum Corps World*, all of whom have so graciously contributed several of the photographs contained within this work. I must give particular acknowledgment to Moe Knox, who so generously contributed the majority of the photographs contained in this book and patiently searched his archives for prints and negatives of some special pictures. It is important to note that unless otherwise credited, the photographs presented in this book are courtesy of Moe Knox.

Special thanks to Art Hlywa, James Duplese, Tom Gabianelli, Cheryl Curran, and Vinny Cautadella for their input and contributions toward ensuring the accuracy of the names and narrative of the book. I would like to acknowledge the Board of Directors of the Hurricanes for their enthusiastic support of this project and commitment to its success. Lastly, I would like to thank Erin Vosgien and Caitrin Cunningham of Arcadia Publishing for their guidance as well as their patience in taking me through the process of getting this book to press. Thank you all!

INTRODUCTION

The Connecticut Hurricanes All-Age Drum & Bugle Corps was founded in 1932 and, 87 years later, thrives as one of the finest in the country. Their early history brought them notoriety throughout Connecticut as a parade unit. In 1955, the Hurricanes shifted into the competitive realm of the popular drum and bugle corps activity. Since that transformation, the Hurricanes have captured every major title available and have achieved fame and notoriety on a national level. Their longevity and success stem from their ability to evolve, adapt, and grow as the marching arts activity has evolved into the model it has become in the 21st century, as well as centering the focus of providing a rewarding experience for the membership, expressed in the mission statement as follows:

> It is the mission of the Connecticut Hurricanes to provide a competitive platform on which their members can build successful, healthy lifestyles through music and performance, and to promote artistic excellence. Emphasis is placed on the development of self-esteem, self-motivation, and self-reliance. It encourages teamwork, sportsmanship, civic pride, and contributions of one's best to a group effort, geared toward individual achievement of common goals. It is an education designed to help members become the best they can be. It can be the education of a lifetime!

Today's Connecticut Hurricanes all-age drum & bugle corps is indeed blessed with a rich heritage. It is a heritage defined through the decades by chemistry, continuity, vision, confidence, hard work, commitment, dedication, and most importantly, remaining true to their mission. These are the intangibles the Hurricanes inherently embrace. As they prepare for their next competitive season, as well as many more seasons to follow, it is their steadfast adherence to these values that will serve to sustain their integrity and their elite status as one of the finest all-age drum and bugle corps in the world.

The Connecticut Hurricanes are often announced as "the Pride of Connecticut," and they are just that. The founding fathers of 1932 could never have envisioned that what they had started as a neighborhood drum corps would one day become a world-class organization running amongst the finest drum corps on the planet. They would certainly be proud of the many years of success that have been realized, but they would also be proud of the mediocre seasons, as those served to strengthen the Hurricanes' resolve to strive for excellence. Perhaps more poignantly, they would even be proud of the years of disappointment when, like a prizefighter, they showed true character by how they picked themselves up off the mat in times of challenge, refusing to be broken, determined to survive and never giving in. They would be proud. The Hurricanes are indeed survivors. Every one of the many hundreds of people who have manned the ranks owns a share of the legacy. The organization has enjoyed wonderful periods of success and has overcome some challenging times. The Hurricanes will steadfastly forge ahead towards their 100th year in 2031 and reign as one of the oldest continually operating corps in the DCA (Drum Corps Associates). The tenacity of the Hurricanes emotes from the people, each and every one a fiber of the fabric, advancing the perpetuation of tradition and fellowship. The body of people that has manned "the long green line" over the years also shares a common bond—the thrill of competition, the lasting friendships and the wonderful memories that will stay with them always, all steeped with pride.

In 1964, I was a 14-year-old boy with limited drum corps exposure. On a warm August night of that year, I attended the World Open Drum Corps Championships in Bridgeport, Connecticut. On this evening, I saw the Connecticut Hurricanes in competition for the very first time. I was mesmerized and can honestly say that on this night I became a Hurricane—well, in essence. In reality, I would not officially become a Hurricane until slightly more than a year hence. Fifty-four years have gone by, and the passion I felt that night at the World Open has never waned. In 2004, I was approached to chronicle the history of the Hurricanes, an honor I readily accepted. The result is an all-encompassing compilation of nearly nine decades of Hurricane history.

This book is an extension of that archive and offers an abbreviated, broad view of the Hurricanes history, as told by the many photographs on these pages as well as through the many snippets of pertinent historical facts. As you browse through this pictorial, you will gain a sense of the long journey the Hurricanes have enjoyed and an appreciation of their evolution, their enduring fellowship, and the enormous sense of pride that drives them!

Introducing the Pride of Connecticut, these are the Connecticut Hurricanes.

—John M. Fisher

One

Inception and the Pre-Competitive Years 1932–1954

The first line of the Hurricanes Corps song says, "There is a corps that we all know, that has the greatest drum corps show." Well, that has not always been the case. The Hurricanes had a humble beginning. Not a lot of detail is recorded of those early years, but the charter members built a corps that would, in time, become one of the most recognizable names in the world of drum corps: the Connecticut Hurricanes. It all started a lifetime ago, way back in 1932. The drum corps was organized as the John H. Collins Post Fife, Drum & Bugle Corps from Derby, Connecticut. It is not known who initiated the corps, whether it was the American Legion or simply a group of guys interested in starting a neighborhood drum corps. But in 1932, when a man named Walter H. DeForest donated six fifes, four snare drums, one bass drum, and a pair of cymbals, the organization that would eventually become the Hurricanes was born.

The first songs learned were the "Thunderer March" (how prophetic is that?) and "Semper Fidelis." The year of 1932 was during the height of the Great Depression, and money was an issue; however, funding for uniforms and more equipment was never an obstacle they could not overcome, it was simply a goal requiring discipline, patience, and perseverance. The John H. Collins Post Fife, Drum & Bugle Corps was now in business. It is quite certain the handful of originals would be truly amazed by how long-enduring and successful, as well as how popular, their undertaking would become.

They started out doing what hundreds of American Legion and VFW drum corps all across America did: march in a variety of local parades and accompany the John H. Collins Post to wherever the American Legion conventions were held, all the while growing their savings account. The great fun that they enjoyed was more to do with camaraderie and hijinks than in competition, but for sure, excellence was their focus.

This is the earliest known photograph of the corps. It was snapped as the Collins Post drum corps crossed over the bridge from Shelton into Derby on Memorial Day, May 30, 1936. The photograph captures the corps outfitted in an early uniform of the American Legion: dark-blue khaki pants with a white stripe, a matching dark-blue button-down shirt with a white tie, and an overseas cap. This look was a step up from their very first uniform of 1932, which consisted of a white shirt, black bow tie, and dark trousers. Ever since they were organized in 1932, the corps made do with these modest uniforms, all the while saving their money and looking forward to the day they would purchase new military-style uniforms and upgrade their appearance. (Courtesy of the Hurricane archives.)

Though not yet called the Hurricanes, the forefathers were indeed an impressive sight. Their new uniform, as shown in this photograph from 1937, is in the West Point military style, featuring a blue cadet jacket highlighted by white piping and chrome buttons, a white belt and cross

Here is an early photograph of the John H. Collins Post drum corps on parade in their new uniforms in 1937. The major goal of funding the new uniforms had been reached by the close of the 1936 parade season, and the members eagerly anticipated unveiling them in 1937. The drum corps members had saved their money for five years and achieved the vision of a more professional and dignified appearance that the new uniforms gave them. Mauri Wring was the musical director and had oversight of his staff—a drum sergeant, a bugle sergeant, and a fife sergeant. The military structure of the organization was familiar to many, likely due to the fact that most of the guys were World War I veterans. (Courtesy of the Hurricane archives.)

straps, grey pants, and black shoes, topped by a blue shako with a white plume. (Courtesy of the Hurricane archives.)

The John H. Collins Post Fife Drum & Bugle Corps is shown looking very crisp on parade in Shelton, Connecticut, in this photograph taken on Memorial Day, May 30, 1939. That is drum major Pat Reidy out in front, and Hurricane stalwart Hector Scarpa is at left in the first row. (Courtesy of the Hurricane archives.)

Pat Reidy leads the Collins Post drum corps on parade in Derby, Connecticut, in this picture from 1939. They are shown marching on Route 34 across the Naugatuck River Bridge. Performing in front of family and friends in various parades throughout the Lower Naugatuck Valley was always the most satisfying part of their schedule. (Courtesy of the Hurricane archives.)

This is Harvey Olderman posing in his brand new uniform alongside his wife, Virginia, around 1937. Olderman, a charter member of the drum corps, marched on the field with the Hurricanes through 1985, well into his 88th year. He became the popular figurehead of the Hurricanes as the American flag honor guard captain. He is a Hurricanes Hall of Famer as well as one of six charter members inducted to the World Drum Corps Hall of Fame in 1976. (Courtesy of the Hurricane archives.)

Pictured here on parade is drum major Pat Reidy in 1939. Reidy holds the distinction of serving the longest tenure as lead drum major of the drum corps, from its origin in 1932 through the 1955 season. He is a well-respected figure in Hurricane history and a member of the Hurricanes Hall of Fame. (Courtesy of the Hurricane archives.)

The drum corps on parade here is, in fact, the John H. Collins Post drum corps. Somehow they do not look themselves as they strut their stuff at the American Legion National Convention's Forty and Eight Parade in St. Louis, Missouri, in this photograph from 1954, and they were quite a sight. The Forty and Eight Parade was a much-anticipated annual event of the American Legion National Convention. The name is a reference to railcars used during World War I that typically carried 40 men and 8 horses. It was chosen to make light of those miserable travel accommodations the veterans had endured. The Forty and Eight Society, founded by military veterans in 1920, is a benevolent organization that is devoted to many charitable efforts. The American Legion's Forty and Eight Parades were intended to be fun events and were most noted for the zany costumes worn by the participants; the John H. Collins Post drum corps was no exception. Coconut bras, grass skirts, straw hats, and makeup were the uniform of the day as they enjoyed a riotous time in this event. (Courtesy of the Hurricane archives.)

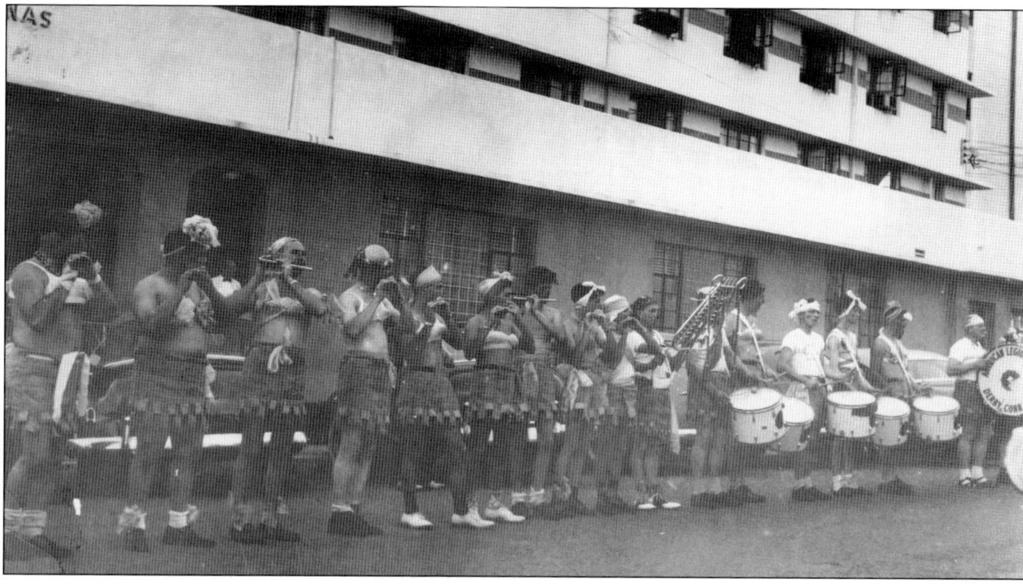

Even with all of the fun, it was not overlooked that one still must perform. In this photograph, the drum corps is shown warming up and preparing to step off in the Forty and Eight Parade in Miami, Florida, in 1951. (Courtesy of the Hurricane archives.)

A few Collins Post boys are pictured here showing off their style in 1951. From left to right, Harry Ogle, George Biancarelli, Gene Imperato, unidentified, Harvey Olderman, and Pat Reidy pose for this picture decked out and ready for the Forty and Eight Parade in Miami, Florida. (Courtesy of the Hurricane archives.)

Throughout Hurricanes history, there are numerous examples of multiple members of one family as well as multiple generations of families becoming members of the Hurricane fellowship. The mounting number of families becoming involved has become commonplace throughout the years. Examples range from immediate family to cousins and in-laws and from aunts and uncles to wives. There have also been several Hurricane marriages. The Hurricanes embrace the family culture in many ways. Shown here are two Hurricanes from the late 1930s with their future Hurricane sons. Ted Yagovane poses with his son Ed (left), while Frank Gabianelli is pictured below with his two sons Frank (left) and Tom. (Left, courtesy of the Yagovane family; below, courtesy of Betty Gabianelli.)

These two full corps photographs are among the scant few pictures from this period in time, dating from the 1930s and 1940s. The photograph above is from the late 1940s, and the one below is from 1951. There is sadness, in hindsight, that the corps lacked the foresight to collect an archive of photographs and memories that would have preserved their early history. (Both, courtesy of the Hurricane archives.)

When the drum corps traveled to Miami, Florida, for the American Legion National Convention in 1951, they enjoyed a rollicking time, so much so that a hotel worker commented that they "brought more chaos than a hurricane!" In taking that comparison as a compliment, they began to unofficially refer to the corps as the "Hurricanes," and the moniker took hold. (Courtesy of the Hurricane archives.)

The Hurricanes are shown as they march up Fifth Avenue in New York City in the American Legion National Convention parade of 1952. Membership was bolstered in the postwar 1940s, and the influx of youth imbued these John H. Collins Post Hurricanes with a swagger and presence that would make them a crowd favorite throughout the region. (Courtesy of the Hurricane archives.)

The image to the right is a page out of James Duplese's scrapbook. The clipping is heralding a first-place finish, Best Drum & Bugle Corps at the VFW parade in Stratford, Connecticut, in 1954. Too few of these mementos have survived, but it is known that a steady stream of acclaim in press clippings, such as this one, gave the corps tremendous confidence as they looked towards the future. The image below illustrates that tremendous confidence as the Hurricanes march down Howe Avenue in Shelton, Connecticut, in 1954. (Both, courtesy of the Hurricane archives.)

Thousands Watch VFW Parade; Prizes Awarded Musical Units

Child's-eye-view of the Derby American Legion post band—snappy uniforms and big bass drum.

Drill Teams Perform

Two floats, a bevy of clowns, precision drilling by the women's auxiliaries, stirring music from the drum corps and bands, and bright uniforms of units like the Governor's Foot Guard delighted viewers who were strung out all along the line of march.

Competition for cash prizes and trophies gave an added sparkle to the proceedings. Winners in the classes limited to VFW units were the Raymond W. Harris post, first in the senior bands; the Lieut. C. C. Robinson post, of Hartford, first in senior drum corps. In the open competitions, the American Legion post of Derby took first in the senior drum corps division, with the Willimantic Cadets, second; the Robert Fletcher post, American Legion, of Norwich, was first in the junior drum corps, and the Stratford PAL and Lincoln school of Bridgeport tied for second; and the PSM band of Milford took first and the Junior Republic of Litchfield, second, in the junior band division.

The Raymond W. Harris post and auxiliary took first prizes for the units with the largest number of members marching. The Harris auxiliary also placed first in the "Best Appearance" competition with the Lieut. C. C. Robinson post of Hartford taking first among the posts.

JUNE 17TH 1954 (STRATFORD) TOOK FIRST PRIZE IN OPEN CLASS SENIORS, DRUM & BUGLE AT VFW CONV
34 MEMBERS 16 BUGLES

Since 1932, the drum corps had done what they did best, performed in parades and had fun doing it, but after World War II, an exciting activity was rapidly expanding and taking hold—field competitions for drum and bugle corps. The John H. Collins Post drum corps naturally wanted to become part of it, and a transformation eventually did take place. The new focus, which would become a reality in 1955, was to train the drum corps that would soon officially be known as the Connecticut Hurricanes for the field as they morphed into a competitive drum and bugle corps. They embraced the challenge. In essence, this photograph captures the Hurricanes marching in the twilight of their parade career, as 1955 would see them embark on a new trajectory and fresh start. (Courtesy of the Hurricane archives.)

Two

Fledgling to Formidable 1955–1969

The first year of competition, 1955, was much like the first year of existence in 1932, though challenging in a different way: new, exciting, and yes, humbling. The bar had been raised, and the Hurricanes soon realized that the level of excellence they aspired to would take a little time. These new, competitive Hurricanes were a far cry from the top-flight drum corps that had inspired them. They needed to learn how to march, and quite a few had to learn to play the bugle. Oscar Knablin was the musical director faced with this daunting task. He had but one player who could actually be considered a musician, 16-year-old Art Hlywa. Hlywa led the way as this group of "green" valley boys made steady strides, playing better and better. It was not long before Hlywa was joined by other pretty good players like Tommy Brady and Joe Giannone. The steady influx of talent had begun. Buddy Ogle was in charge of the drumline in 1955 and subsequently turned it over to the renowned Earl Sturtze in 1956; it was quickly turned into a respectable unit. Perhaps one of the best marching instructors of the day, Vinnie Ratford, was in charge of the drill. The Hurricanes of 1955 were a neighborhood corps, and they competed in the Yankee Circuit against drum corps from Connecticut, Rhode Island, and Massachusetts of a similar caliber that rendered a level playing field. The Hurricanes achieved modest success in 1955. They took some lumps in this inaugural year but also beat a few corps along the way and actually notched their first contest victory that year.

In 1955, the Hurricanes took to the field of competition. Here is the full corps photograph of that trailblazing core of originals taken in May 1955. Pictured in this image from the inaugural year are, from left to right (first row) Bucky Welch, Don Zuleger, Frank Ogle, Harry Ogle, Buzzy McCarrick, Karl Krebs, Joe Latton, Gene Waradzin, Bob Woods, Buddy Ogle, and George Waradzin; (second row) Lou Mattei, Gerry Moscariello, Dom Margiano, Art Martin, Joe Balint, Bill Brennan, Dick Pagano, Ed McGarry, Ed McManus, and Don Klanko; (third row) Art Hlywa, Dick Sill, Bob Rose, Ed Condon, Bob Stevens, Richard Donofrio, Ed Mongillo, Frank Gabianelli, and Dick Benham; (fourth row) drum major Pat Reidy, color captain Hector Scarpa, Henry Osak, Charlie McManus, Joe Ragucki, Harvey Olderman, Ted Yagovane, and director Gene Imperato. (Courtesy of the Hurricane archives.)

The Hurricanes are shown on parade in this photograph from 1956. That is color guard captain Jim Duplese leading the American flag honor guard and drum major Eddie Welles in front of the drum corps. (Courtesy of the Hurricane archives.)

This image depicts the Hurricanes "breaking through" on the cover of the program book for the competition they sponsored in 1956. The imagery was not off the mark, as the Hurricanes were indeed a rising star in the Yankee Circuit in just their second year. (Courtesy of the Hurricane archives.)

Pictured here are the 1957 Hurricanes. By the third year of competition, the Hurricanes' star was shining bright in the Yankee Circuit. They closed out this season by entering the American Legion Nationals, which were held in Atlantic City, New Jersey, on September 14, 1957. A 19th-place finish did not dampen their spirit, for they had experienced a taste of the big time, and it energized them going forwards. (Courtesy of the Hurricane archives.)

Color guard captain Jim Duplese (left) leads the honor guard as they march on parade in 1957. This picture is among the final images showing the Hurricanes walking proudly in the uniform that served them so well for over two decades. A makeover was imminent, and their new look would capture the essence of the Hurricanes identity. (Courtesy of the Hurricane archives.)

The arrival of Joe Genero (right) in 1957 marked the onset of a 20-year odyssey that ushered in the Hurricanes' rise to prominence. Under Genero's guidance as musical director, the Hurricanes would garner several championship titles and flourish as an elite DCA corps. By way of his accomplishments with the Hurricanes and through the impact he achieved teaching numerous units throughout the Northeast, Genero became a drum corps icon and Hurricane legend. Pictured below is featured performer and assistant horn instructor Art Hlywa suiting up for a performance in 1959. Hlywa reigned as the cornerstone of the Hurricane horn line for 17 years and also instructed several drum corps throughout Connecticut. Both of these staunch Hurricanes have earned induction to the Hurricanes Hall of Fame as well as to the World Drum Corps Hall of Fame. (Below, courtesy of Annette Hlywa.)

In 1958, with continued resolve to make their mark and command the respect of the drum corps community, the Hurricanes were once again sporting new uniforms. The drum corps sealed their identity with a new look consisting of a black jacket, black pants with a white stripe, white shoes, black military hat with a chrome medallion at the peak, and the feature that would become the most recognizable for the Hurricanes: a silver lightning bolt across their chests. Just as in 1937, these new uniforms generated enormous pride. The photograph above captures the Hurricanes performing in Agawam, Massachusetts, in 1958. The Hurricanes captured the Yankee Circuit Championship in 1958 playing a show featuring tunes including "Stormy Weather," "Rain," "Basin Street Blues," "Muskrat Ramble," and "I'll Never Smile Again."

The new identity looked great, and the lightning bolt was here to stay. This photograph is of the Hurricanes American flag honor guard in 1958. Pictured from left to right are captain Jim Duplese, Bob Daniels, future director Peter Burns, Dick Burns, George Miller, Dick Sauer, Harvey Olderman, and two unidentified men.

This embroidery depicts the official logo of the Hurricanes that was adopted in 1958 and adorned the new uniforms on the left chest. It consists of red hurricane warning flags blowing in the wind on a white shield, slashed by a vivid green lightning bolt. Traditionally presented without a name, the logo has become so recognizable throughout the drum corps community that it is instantly identified with the Connecticut Hurricanes. (Courtesy of the Hurricane archives.)

A very popular and prominent feature of the Hurricane uniform for nearly 40 years was this military-style hat. The marching members loved this hat, feeling it gave the drum corps a look that meant business as well as a look of gravitas.

In 1956, the Hurricanes moved to Shelton, Connecticut, and the sponsorship of Sutter-Terlizzi American Legion Post 16. Shown here is some of the hardware from 1958, including the newly captured Yankee Circuit Championship flag of 1958.

In 1956, a plaque was presented to director Gene Imperato in appreciation of his many years of dedicated service. Imperato, a 1932 original, had imparted a huge influence on the evolution of the Hurricanes. He is credited with having the foresight and "can do" mind-set to oversee the transformation of the drum corps from a parade unit to a competitive drum and bugle corps in 1955. Standing from left to right are Ted Yagovane, George Biancarelli, Imperato, Jimmy Duplese, and Pat Reidy. (Courtesy of the Hurricane archives.)

The Hurricanes are on the starting line on June 14, 1959, in Hamden, Connecticut. Achieving mastery of the military style of marching that prevailed in this era required many hours of rehearsal dedicated to practicing an exercise known as eights and eights to gain the knack of marching in and maintaining straight lines. The 1959 repertoire included such songs as "Stormy Weather," "Rain," "Battle Hymn of the Republic," "Autumn Leaves," "A Foggy Day in London Town," and "Tropical Heatwave."

On September 10, 1961, the Hurricanes performed before a crowd of 50,373 people as the halftime show for a New York Giants–Baltimore Colts preseason game that was played in the Yale Bowl in New Haven, Connecticut.

The Hurricanes enjoyed their growing notoriety and reigned as crowd-pleasers at the many local parades where they appeared. Shown here in 1961 leading the Hurricanes on parade are color guard captain Peter Burns (left) and sergeant Harvey Olderman (right).

The Hurricanes are pictured on parade in Bridgeport, Connecticut, in 1961. That year, a filler song was added to the repertoire that was so well received it would become the Hurricanes' signature song—the theme from *The Magnificent Seven*, commonly referred to as "Mag 7."

In this photograph, the Hurricanes are shown performing at a spring preview show in the New Haven Arena on April 2, 1962, where they unveiled new tunes for the upcoming season: "They Call the Wind Maria," a medly of "Maria" and "Tonight," and "Till the Clouds Roll By." That is drum major Bob Daniels in front directing.

This photograph shows the Hurricanes at Carnegie Hall in New York City, where they appeared in 1963, 1964, and 1965 as regular participants of An Evening with the Corps. In 1963, they premiered new tunes for their show, including "Mutiny on the Bounty," "Tonight," "Battle Hymn of the Republic," "Bill Bailey, Won't You Please Come Home?", and "Love Look Away." Future venues for this popular event were Symphony Hall in Newark, New Jersey, and the Felt Forum in New York City.

Pictured is the ever-popular Bobby Daniels, Hurricane drum major from 1958 through 1963. Daniels led the Hurricanes as they ascended the drum corps ladder in a style that was often described as "flashy." He would return to his corps in 1969 and 1970 and again in 1975 and 1976 as the drill designer/instructor to drive and motivate the Hurricanes in his inimitable fiery way.

Shown on parade in 1963, the Hurricanes step smartly in new uniforms featuring black pants replete with a white stripe edged in green piping and a white satin blouse adorned by a lime-green sequin cummerbund and a sequin lightning bolt across the chest, topped with the same black military-style hat they had been sporting. These uniforms created a striking presence; in a word, they were electrifying.

The quartermaster corps has always been an unheralded element of the drum corps. They transport and maintain all of the equipment and uniforms, line stripe practice fields, provide water, Band-Aids, and aspirin, and tend to many other necessary needs. It was simpler times when this van served as the corps' equipment truck. In today's world, this truck would barely fit the podiums. Pictured here in 1964 are, from left to right, quartermasters George Biancarelli, Tony Montanaro, and Charlie Matula.

In the fall of 1963, the concept of a new circuit to be called Drum Corps Associates (DCA) came into being. DCA marked its first year with a full competitive schedule in 1964. In this picture, the Hurricanes look poised and confident as they stand at the ready on the starting line in 1964. "Hello Dolly," "Under the Double Eagle," and "Tropical Heatwave" were popular tunes in the repertoire.

On August 30, 1964, the Hurricanes stunned the drum corps world by winning the Senior World Open Championship. Pictured in this image are, from left to right, director and color guard captain Peter Burns alongside beaming drum major Joe Genero, Bridgeport Catholic Youth Organization director Rev. Louis DeProfio, and World Open director Raymond Samora as they present the World Open Championship flag. Since transitioning to a competitive unit in 1955, the Hurricanes had risen to the pinnacle of the drum corps world in 10 short years.

The drumline under the guidance of percussion guru Ray Luedee was, of course, a key element of the competition formula during the rise to prominence. Pictured here is a segment of the Hurricane drum line in action in 1966.

The Barnum Festival parade in Bridgeport, Connecticut, took place in sweltering heat registering 100 degrees on July 4, 1966, driving these thirsty Hurricanes to a water fountain spotted along the parade route. Shown clockwise from left are Matty Moales (taking a drink), Tom Wallace, John Tarantino, Bob Glovna, Jack Smith, Ron Dubois, Rowland Libby, unidentified, Jim Donnely, Milton "Whispers" LaBonte, Bobby Chop, Dennis Brady, and Albert "Moose" George (bottom right).

The Hurricanes of 1966 were mighty competitors as they continued their winning ways with eight trips to the winners' circle, six second places, and one third. In the above image, drum major Joe Genero (left) is captured directing the concert number "Tropical Heatwave" on the DC Stadium field in Washington, DC, on August 18, 1966. In the photograph below, the American flag honor section guards the colors at the National Dream contest on August 21, 1966, in Jersey City, New Jersey. Pictured from left to right Jimmy Edgeworth, Whitey Ziomek, Marv Hosenfeld, Ray Ruff, Tony DeFrancesco, Eddie Melfi, and sergeant Harvey Olderman.

The Hurricanes of 1967 had a stellar year, winning nine contests while placing second but twice, with victories in prestigious shows such as Mission Drums, the Barnum Festival, and the National Dream contest as well as capturing the American Legion National Championship and DCA World Championship titles. (Courtesy of the Hurricane archives.)

Gathering the trophies on August 27, 1967, at the American Legion Nationals at Fenway Park in Boston are the newly crowned national champion Hurricanes. Standing from left to right are drum major Joe Genero, director and color guard captain Peter Burns, color guard sergeant Harvey Olderman, and drum major Tony DeFrancesco.

A proud and exuberant Hurricane color guard exits the award ceremonies of the American Legion Nationals in 1967 carrying the orange flag of the champions. The Hurricanes powered through the season with a repertoire featuring "The Man I Love," "Start Off Each Day with a Song," "Just One of Those Songs," "Under the Double Eagle," "National Emblem March," "America I Love You," "Rhapsody in Blue," "Fiddler on the Roof," "Return of the Magnificent Seven," and "Stormy Weather."

A very satisfied expression is on the faces of the drumline as they stand on retreat at the Legion Nationals in 1967. Standing from left to right are John Bodnar, Jim Donnely, Tom Wallace, Ray Luedee, Bob Moravek, Jim Crowley, Max Stewart, Dave Collins, Dave Bartrum, and Jackie Lester; Dave Ruot and Bob Laskowsky stand in front on the bass drums.

Drum major Joe Genero (left) and color guard sergeant Harvey Olderman (right) share a moment at the 1967 American Legion Nationals in Boston. The Hurricanes were crowned national champions at this show on August 27, 1967.

Ed Condon and Bob Woods, mentored by Vinny Ratford, succeeded him as drill designers/instructors in the early 1960s. Under their tutelage, the Hurricanes enjoyed a marching prowess that was unparalleled throughout the decade. In the military style of marching, the eyes looked right, left, diagonally, or straight in order to keep formations dressed. The steely eyed look of concentration is evident as "Pittsburgh" Dave Younkin bears down in 1968.

When there was idle time prior to a parade, the boys always seemed to find a way to have a few laughs. In 1968, Victor Poulan takes one for the corps as he "falls" on the flag (left). In another skit, Victor the "drum major" leads George "Freddy McKermish" Clendenon on parade to the delight of all onlookers.

The Hurricanes of 1969 are shown performing at the Barnum Festival competition in Bridgeport, Connecticut, on July 5. They would place fourth on this night but would subsequently run out the season in first place, thus capturing their second DCA World Championship. Musical selections included *Les Preludes* Overture, *Queen of Sheba* March, *Hallelujah* Chorus, "Rhapsody in Blue," "Walk on the Wild Side," "Hang 'Em High," "The Magnificent Seven," and "Also Sprach Zarathustra."

The final statement of the 1969 show featured a 60-yard company front executed to a haunting rendition of "Hang 'Em High" that transitioned into the Hurricanes signature song, "The Magnificent Seven." Maintaining a straight line was key to the success of this maneuver, and the boys usually achieved it.

Led by drum major Joe Genero, seen here, the Hurricanes capped the decade of the 1960s by celebrating their second DCA World Championship. The 1969 season, as magical and rewarding as it became, was in effect an exclamation point on the entire decade. The Hurricanes closed out the 1960s having gone into competition against 54 opponents. Of those, only 16 corps managed to outscore the men from Connecticut on occasion. The Hurricanes took the field of competition 108 times and placed first 52 times and second 24 times. That's an amazing record for the era; in fact, the Hurricanes were the only corps with a winning record against every corps that took the field of competition against them over that 10-year period, culminating with the last of many titles amassed during the decade: their second DCA World Championship.

Three

THOSE WILD 1970s
1970–1979

As they flipped the calendar to the 1970s, the Hurricanes maintained their stature as a top-flight contender with indefatigable competition against the best of the best. It is a great boost to the ego to be introduced to a crowd as the reigning champions, as they were in 1970, and this enhanced the great vibe permeating the Hurricanes as they looked toward the future. Joe Genero and longtime drum arranger/instructor Ray Luedee kept churning out one popular show after another. Coming off the fabulous run of the 1960s only gave the members the desire to continue their winning ways. In the first half of the decade, the Hurricanes were as intense, as powerful, as competitive, and as entertaining as always but nonetheless failed to win another championship. The competition was extremely tough, and the Hurricanes were always in the mix, but the top spot in the big shows proved elusive.

By the mid-1970s, the drum corps landscape had undergone drastic change, not only in Connecticut but across the country. Junior corps had, one by one, gone inactive, thus leaving the Hurricanes with a deeply depleted pool for recruitment opportunities. At the close of 1976, this became an issue when a large number of Hurricane veterans had reached their time to leave. Membership dipped, creating a crisis that would need to be addressed. This was an extremely pivotal period in the history of drum corps, and effectively adapting to the paradigm shift would take years to understand and achieve.

The Hurricanes shine in the spotlight as they perform in the popular annual spring preview show, An Evening with the Corps, which was presented at the Felt Forum in New York City on May 16, 1970. That is drum major Jim McHenry directing. He would lead the Hurricanes to a third-place finish in the DCA Championships with a score of 80.95.

The Hurricanes are pictured here in front of a full house at the Barnum Festival in Bridgeport, Connecticut, on their way to a first-place finish on July 5, 1970. Popular song selections from that year included a medley from *Sweet Charity*, including "If They Could See Me Now" and "I'm a Brass Band," followed by a jazzy version of "The Stars and Stripes Forever."

All elements of the corps were strong, and the drumline was no exception (above). They were a perennial strength and excelled. Pictured below heading towards the starting line for competition is the snare line of 1970, from left to right, John Bodnar, Ray Luedee, Tom Gabianelli, Ken Convertito, and Jim Donnely.

Pictured on this page are the Hurricanes at the Barnum Festival in 1971. A spirited performance by a highly motivated Hurricane corps resulted in a second-place finish on this night. The 1971 Hurricanes would outscore every competitor they faced in that year on occasion and ended a hard-fought campaign in third place at the DCA Championship contest.

The Hurricanes are shown above entering the competition field at the Barnum Festival on July 3, 1971, in a compact formation before bursting across the field to the strains of "If They Could See Me Now" and "I'm a Brass Band." A lightning bolt formation, below, was utilized for an effective presentation of a powerful rendition of "Malaguena," the concert selection of 1971.

Here is drum major "Jumpin' Joe" Genero in front in this photograph of the Hurricanes in 1972, perhaps the largest and most powerful Hurricane corps of all. The Hurricanes competed in 14 contests in 1972 and placed second nine times. They would ultimately finish tied for fourth place in the DCA Championship contest with what are considered by many to be the greatest top five corps in DCA history.

As the Hurricanes march on parade in New Haven's St. Patrick's Day parade in 1972, an adoring fan cannot resist an opportunity and breaks the ranks for an up-close look. Might he be a future Hurricane? The captivating Hurricane is soprano stalwart Curt Golder.

Here are two more photographs of the 1972 Hurricanes that convey the intensity they displayed with their high-energy show that year. "Fanfare for the New," "Fiddler on the Roof," "Malaguena," "The Impossible Dream," "America the Beautiful," "Rule Britannia," "La Marseillaise," "Fanfare for the Common Man," "Hang 'Em High," "The Magnificent Seven," and "Also Sprach Zarathustra" rounded out the musical selections highlighting the powerful presentation of 1972.

The Hurricanes are once again shown performing at the Barnum Festival on June 30, 1973. Kennedy Stadium in Bridgeport, Connecticut, was always a favorite venue for the Hurricanes, as it had a welcoming hometown atmosphere and was a great stadium for panoramic photographs.

This picture captures the Hurricanes as they execute their hugely effective "suicide wheel" to the pulsing strains of "Hang 'Em High," a maneuver that never failed to delight the appreciative crowds. The wheel became a signature maneuver for the Hurricanes in the 1970s.

The 1973 color guard was in high Hurricane fashion as they carried their signature "Hurricane Storm Warning" flags.

Uniformity is the appropriate caption for this 1973 photograph. Pictured from left to right are Rocky Baglio, Arnie Juliano, Tony Convertito, Paul Kasperzyk, Al Richmond, Bob Rawden, Tony LoPresti, and Bob Findley.

This photograph shows the climax of the 1973 show, known as the re-entry. The Hurricanes turned around backfield and, with drum major Tom Hart leading the way, stormed across the field playing "The Billboard March," with the drums thundering and the horns blazing. The re-entry proved to be a mighty finish to a high-energy show.

Complexity and precision are unique features of drill designs. Well-crafted designs are necessary to present the musical program in the most effective and impactful way. This photograph shows the 1974 Hurricanes playing their closing number, "The Way We Were."

Not all ideas are good ones. This picture from 1974 shows the Hurricanes leaving the field following the final note of "Stormy Weather," hoisting small umbrellas as if it were really raining. This turned out to be a bad idea that was only done once. Mark Paul is captured enjoying the misguided moment.

Pictured here is Ray Luedee, the man who arranged, taught, and led the Hurricane drumline for 13 years. Luedee produced drum lines that were the muscle of the Hurricanes that placed at or near the top of the percussion caption consistently from 1965 through 1977. His accomplished drum corps career has been honored and acknowledged through induction to the Hurricanes Hall of Fame as well as to the World Drum Corps Hall of Fame.

The 1975 Hurricanes made a statement entering the field with a 50-yard company front to the peppy melody of "I Got Rhythm." The final tune of the show included the attention-grabbing suicide wheel as well. These two maneuvers confirmed that all of those tedious eights and eights, the mainstay of marching exercises, paid off.

The 1975 Hurricanes are shown here performing at the Barnum Festival in Bridgeport, Connecticut, on July 5. The Hurricanes delighted the very savvy hometown crowd as they moved up in the rankings, powering to a second-place finish on this day.

The year 1975 was one of intensity that left every Hurricane who manned the ranks with indelible fond memories. The Hurricanes began the season in last place in their first contest with a score of 59.23 and subsequently clawed their way to a fourth-place finish at the DCA finals with a score of 86.98. Pictured above is the snare line of 1975; from left to right are Vic Kulinski, Steve Cassidy, Ray Crowthers, Danny Alcutt, and Bill Palumbo, while the photograph to the right shows drum major Al Richmond in action as he led that gritty edition of the Hurricanes through a most rewarding season.

The Hurricanes had long ago ceased being a neighborhood drum corps. Competitive success and notoriety throughout the drum corps community attracted members to the Hurricanes from all across the Northeast. Pictured is the "Boston Crew" of 1975; from left to right are (first row, kneeling) John Curran, Fuzzy Vorel, and Paul Gaffney; (second row, standing) Henry "Chris" Dunn, John Gebaur, and Howie Sederquist. Absent from the photograph is John Gore.

There was also a group from upstate New York on the roster in 1975. Known as the "Syracuse Crew," it was comprised of guys from the Hudson Valley area as well as the Syracuse region; From left to right are (first row, kneeling) Mike Morano, Wayne Norman, Bob Curtiss, Milton "Whispers" Labonte, and Neal VanDusen; (second row, standing) John Brannigan, Carl Pynn, Gary Ferris, Steve Smith, and Mike Mysek.

In 1976, the drill design lent itself nicely to a soprano feature backed by solid percussion (above), while a cloud of balloons released during the finale of "Stars and Stripes Forever" triggered very satisfying audience responses for this patriotic bicentennial salute. The year 1976, however, ended in disappointment as the Hurricanes finished the season in the DCA Championship in a distant sixth place with a score of 79.95.

In the wake of the 1976 season, an unusual number of veterans reached their time to retire. The prospect of gaining new members was limited. The nucleus of the corps shrank drastically. In essence, this was the end of an era. The Hurricanes were faced with two compelling issues: rebuilding the horn line and recognizing the evolutionary turn color guards had taken. A revolutionary plan to revitalize the Hurricanes by creating a new, all-female color guard was enacted, hence the "Men from Connecticut" transformed into "the Pride of Connecticut." In addition, the members of the old color guard transferred to the brass and percussion sections, thus solving the dilemma. Today, the resolution to make the Hurricanes coed seems as if it would be a no-brainer, but in 1976, it was a monumental decision. Pictured here are some original members of the new female color guard; from left to right are (first row, kneeling) Marie Kane; (second row, standing) Brenda Curran, Heidi King, Laura Lally, Leta Golder, and Fran Kulpowich.

The membership crisis of 1977 certainly had a silver lining, as the new Hurricane color guard proved to be a wonderful addition to the drum corps, not just in 1977 but throughout the decades that would follow. The image above shows the rifle line of 1977 in action, while Nancy Wilcox, one of the inaugural members of new Hurricanes that year, is pictured at right. The Hurricanes finished the season in a distant eighth place in the DCA finals with a score of 78.60, but the focus on the future remained fixed.

The off-season may lack the luster of competition but is, nonetheless, equally important. Learning new material, as well as the anticipation of unveiling it in the spring, is eagerly embraced. The three Hurricanes shown in this image honing their skills in the winter of 1978 are, from left to right, Bob Bradley, Johnny Glynn, and Doug Oravez. The image below shows the Hurricanes in action in 1978. (Above, courtesy of Gary W. Ferris.)

Drum major Dave MacLennan mans the podium as he directs a percussion feature in 1978 (above). The makeover of the previous year resulted in a refreshed mind-set, with the membership eager to excel. All elements of the drum corps—brass, percussion, and color guard—were now coed, and camaraderie and enthusiasm began to gel. The popular tunes from *Star Wars* comprised a show that brought the Hurricanes back into the top five. Pictured to the right are three members of the rifle line punctuating a high point of that show; from left to right are Donna Broadbent, Diana MacLennan, and JoAnn Orris.

The Hurricanes had weathered a rough stretch and soon re-established themselves as a premier DCA corps with a return to the coveted top five via fifth-place finishes in 1978 and 1979. The 1979 Hurricanes are shown on this page. Their repertoire of "Children of Sanchez," "Sgt. Pepper's Lonely Hearts Club Band," "Got to Get You into My Life," "Nowhere Man," and "The Magnificent Seven" brought them a score of 78.65 and fifth place at the DCA Championship contest.

Four

From the Mountain Top to the Valley 1980–1989

The new decade saw a continuation of the Hurricanes' ascension. The membership had become a close-knit group that possessed great chemistry and focus. The Hurricanes showed their true mettle as they clawed their way up in the rankings and sealed the 1980 season with a third-place showing at the DCA Championship contest. The year also saw the Hurricanes change to new uniforms. Bill Duquette had been named director and promptly unveiled a new look for the drum corps. The uniform consisted of a white cadet-style jacket replete with hunter-green piping, pants with red and gold stripes, a red and gold shimmering cummerbund, and a sash with a lightning bolt, topped with the traditional Hurricane military hat in white and white shoes.

The 1981 competition season began slowly for the Hurricanes. As the reigning champions, the Reading Buccaneers were the corps to beat. After a slow start to begin the season, the Hurricanes began realizing the results of a grueling rehearsal schedule of four and sometimes five days a week, as they began to move up in the rankings. The drum corps really began to gel. Scores became tighter, and posting late-season placements of one first, four seconds, and two third-place showings positioned the Hurricanes for a shot at a big win. The Hurricanes worked relentlessly in preparing for the DCA Championships in Philadelphia. They went into the championship weekend with confidence and control. Preliminary competition results had the Hurricanes in first, and in the finals, they responded with an electrifying performance, the yield of so many weeks of extraordinary perseverance; it was a performance that resulted with the Hurricanes capturing their third DCA Championship crown. The rebuilding effort over the past five years was ultimately very gratifying indeed.

The Hurricanes unveiled their new uniforms on Memorial Day in 1980. Shown here on parade looking pressed and crisp are, from left to right, Doug Oravez, Larry MacClennan, and Mark Burell. The iconic Hurricane storm warning logo would soon be added to the left chest to complete the look. (Courtesy of the Hurricane archives.)

The Hurricane color guard also stepped out looking great in their new uniforms on Memorial Day in 1980. They would go on that year to a very memorable season.

"Eyes front" would be a perfect caption for this picture, as this Hurricane could not resist taking a moment for a sneak peek at his drum corps sporting a fresh Hurricane look in 1980. (Courtesy of Ann Marie Fisher and the Hurricane archives.)

"Hurcs Win DCA!" was the headline above this photograph on the front page of *Drum Corps World* in 1981. It captures an exuberant Robert "Pepe" Notaro displaying approval of the title-winning performance in Philadelphia. Notaro, Ray Fallon, Mickey Kelly, Dennis Banks, Neal Smith, Gus Barbaro, Tony Palumbo, and more headed an impressive, hard-driving instructional staff that prepared the Hurricanes well and led them into the winner's circle that year. (Courtesy of *Drum Corps World*.)

The Hurricanes are shown on the starting line for the DCA Championships at Franklin Field in Philadelphia on September 6, 1981, where they would capture their third DCA crown. *Queen of Sheba* March, "When Johnny Comes Marching Home," "Swing, Swing, Swing," and "It's My Turn" were the tunes rounding out this championship effort.

Pictured above is Dodie Wynn leading the rifle line and color guard off the field following retreat ceremonies in 1981. The 16-member rifle line of 1981 was nothing short of fabulous and added a dimension to the overall production that was hard to top.

Hurricane director and drum major Bill Duquette accepts the first-place trophy for the newly crowned DCA World Champion Hurricanes in 1981. Pictured from left to right are George Parks, drum major of the bronze medalist Reading Buccaneers; Duquette; Tony White, drum major of the runner-up Sunrisers; and Vince Bruni, DCA president.

Following their championship season of 1981, the Hurricanes were once again very strong in 1982. With another show of popular selections including *Rustic Wedding* Overture, "Moonlight Serenade," "Swing, Swing, Swing," "Salute to Freedom," "Let It Be Me," and "The Magnificent Seven," the Hurricanes were again very competitive and ended the season with a third-place finish in the DCA Championships. Pictured are the Hurricanes on the field in 1982.

Parades have long been the lifeblood of the Hurricanes by delivering much-needed revenue. In the image above, the Hurricanes are shown on parade in 1983, while the image below captures Beth Donna out in front of the color guard as they lead the corps on parade in 1984.

The drumline stands at parade rest while on retreat on July 14, 1984, in East Rutherford, New Jersey. The retreat ceremony is the closing formality of a drum corps competition where the awards are presented. The Hurricanes would place third on this night and would ultimately go on to a sixth-place finish at the DCA Championship contest, scoring an 83.25.

Pictured in their inaugural year of 1984 is the Connecticut Alumni Drum & Bugle Corps. They were conceived of and organized by George Biancarelli and John Fisher in 1984. Initially comprised primarily of Hurricanes, the Alumni flourishes today and has maintained a strong Hurricane identity for 35 years and counting. The Hurricanes and the Alumni drum corps share a mutual respect and partner in promoting drum corps in the Naugatuck Valley in addition to actively supporting each other.

The Hurricanes of 1984 were led by drum major Vic Kulinski. Musical selections of "Meadowland," *Pictures at an Exhibition*, "Gumbie Cats," "Rhapsody in Blue," and "The Magnificent Seven" rounded out the show. Kulinski not only manned the center podium as lead drum major through 1989 but also served as the Hurricanes' director from 1986 through 1989 and had the unenviable task of guiding the Hurricanes through some very stormy weather. The photograph below captures the Hurricanes on the field of competition in 1984.

With a repertoire of "Olympic Fanfare," "Imagination," "Don't Leave Me," "I Loved These Days," and "The Magnificent Seven" in 1985, the Hurricanes finished the season in a distant ninth place with a score of 74.05. The full corps photograph above, as well as a noticeably smaller drum line as pictured below, depicts a sharp contrast from years past. Competing with a smaller corps presented challenges on many levels that would subsequently nag the Hurricanes in the days to come.

Following the 1985 season, shrinking membership became a concern. A strong nucleus and dedicated leadership would be paramount to weather the challenges facing the Hurricanes. A major water leak at the Hurricanes' home ruined the uniform jackets. Without funding, director Vic Kulinski scrambled to replace them. The replacement consisted of a black waiter's jacket trimmed with silver, worn over a silver ascot emblazoned with a lightning bolt, white pants, green cummerbund, and white hats. The jackets were donated by a local linen company, the pants were purchased at an Army/Navy store, and the hats were graciously provided, at cost, by a uniform supply company. On a sad note, in October 1985, the Hurricane family lost an icon. Harvey Olderman, seen here, passed away at the age of 88, leaving a void as well as a legacy of class and dedication. An original member in 1932, he had become the most recognizable figurehead of the Hurricanes over 54 consecutive years of performing with the corps.

In 1986, the Hurricanes repertoire consisted of "Concerto to End All Concertos," "Catavento," "Return of the Magnificent Seven," "They Call the Wind Maria," "The Greatest Love of All," and "The Magnificent Seven." Pictured are the make-shift uniforms hastily assembled for the 1986 season.

This photograph shows the color guard uniforms of 1986: kelly-green jackets trimmed with silver sequins boldly highlighting a basic white outfit. Pictured in white leading the guard is color guard captain Mary Kantorowski.

Pictured in this image is the snare line of 1986, which includes stalwarts, from left to right, Dave Dion, Bob Kogut, John Ashelford, and Bill Gregor. Of this group, Dion and Kogut would go on to noteworthy Hurricane careers as arrangers and instructors, as would Ashelford, who in 2012 became chairman of the Board of Directors of the Hurricanes.

Despite a concerted effort by a smaller corps in 1986, the Hurricanes would finish the season in a disappointing 12th place at the championships that year with a score of 73.40, thus falling out of the top 10 in 1986 for the first time since DCA's inception.

Shown on this page are the 1987 Hurricanes. The show consisted of "The Theme from an *American Tail*," "Market Street," "Begin the Beguine," "They Call the Wind Maria," and "The Magnificent Seven." A diligent effort by the Hurricanes resulted in a return to the top 10 in 1987 with a score of 82.64, which was good for 10th place. As these photographs show, the uniforms were gradually being upgraded with better-quality accessories. The cost for new uniforms at this point in time was prohibitive, so upgrades to the uniform would need to be incremental.

A constant over the decade was brass arranger/instructor Ray Fallon. In a Hurricane career that earned induction to the Hurricanes Hall of Fame as well as the World Drum Corps Hall of Fame, Fallon penned the brass arrangements for 10 editions of the Hurricanes, proving invaluable through his influence and the even-keeled mentorship he imparted from the heady days of a championship run to the stormy years of the second half of the decade. (Courtesy of the Hurricane archives.)

By 1989, the Hurricanes had shown considerable improvement, both in their level of performance and through an upgraded appearance. They had weathered the challenging storms over the past six years due to a tenacious membership and the steely determination of the leadership.

Five

Resurgence 1990–1999

The dawn of a new decade brought with it optimism and promise. The Hurricanes felt they had weathered the storm—hooray for those dedicated members! They had survived the challenges of those dark days and the uncertainty that plagued the Hurricanes during the second half of the 1980s. They had refused to cave and had persevered by riding the will and pride of a small nucleus and saved the Hurricanes from extinction. This gritty group of survivors gave new meaning to the mantra "walk proud and tall" and had every reason to do just that.

The year 1990 brought the return of Bob Bradley into the fold as executive director with Bill Duquette returning to assume the duties of administrative head and show/program coordinator. To add to the excitement, a new uniform was unveiled. The uniform consisted of a white cadet-style jacket with red piping and a black lapel, folded down from the breast panel. A red sash crossed the chest with a green cummerbund on the waist. It was topped by a black shako with a green plume, black pants and shoes, and not to be overlooked, black gauntlets bearing the signature lightning bolt.

Beginning in 1990, many veterans returning to the Hurricanes gave them a necessary—if only temporary—lift. Not to be misunderstood, these people performed as they had in the past: at a level of excellence they clearly understood. They were, however, only a Band-Aid. A solution for sustaining continuous recruiting opportunities remained elusive. Thus, when the veterans eventually trickled out, their numbers and talent could not easily be replaced. Recruiting efforts geared toward local school bands was yielding limited results. A formal strategy for recruiting had yet to be developed and would take time to refine and mature. But for the moment, the Hurricanes were on the rise!

It was about this period in time when the evolution of drum corps obliged corps to tailor their shows to a theme. The theme of the 1990 corps was "Pictures at an Exhibition," a good show that ultimately garnered 10th place at the DCA Championships in Allentown, Pennsylvania. Was it a great corps? No, but the Hurricanes were certainly respectable and used 1990 as a springboard for some satisfying seasons to come.

The Hurricanes were resplendent in their new uniforms and eagerly marched into the fresh decade with invigoration as well as a freshened resolve to reclaim their stature in the upper echelon of the DCA. In this photograph, the retooled Hurricanes are walking proud as they enter the field in 1990.

Pictured here in 1990 is the drumline looking and sounding solid. This crowd-pleasing show featured selections of "A Night on Bald Mountain," *Pictures at an Exhibition*, "Swing Street," "Cleanin' Up the Town," "Wind Beneath My Wings," and "The Magnificent Seven," which energized the Hurricanes.

The new uniforms of 1990 looked great and added a little extra spring to the step. Shown in the photograph above front and center is Hurricanes director Bob Bradley on parade. The image below captures the two able frontmen for the resurgent Hurricanes of 1990 in veteran drum majors David MacClennan (left) and George Maloney (right).

The theme for 1991 was "Magic," with musical selections including "Bewitched, Bothered and Bewildered," "That Old Black Magic," "Umulu," and *Symphonie Fantastique* and in addition featured the color guard and front percussion ensemble outfitted in theme-related costume. That is drum major George Maloney on the podium directing the Hurricanes. The Hurricanes made their return to the coveted top five in 1991 at the DCA Championships with a score of 90.50.

The featured performer on the trap set in this photograph is none other than Dave Dion. Dion enjoyed a wonderful playing career prior to a stint as lead drum major of the Hurricanes. He would subsequently serve as the percussion arranger/instructor for 11 years, and he also penned the brass arrangements for two years. He was inducted into the Hurricanes Hall of Fame in recognition of his very special 23-year Hurricanes career of prominence.

This picture from 1991 illustrates the challenges endured due to a less-than-reliable bus company. It is a good thing the many hours on the practice field kept the members fit, as it sometimes required a group effort to stay on schedule. (Courtesy of Cheryl Curran.)

Musical selections for 1992 featured "Gospel John," "Make His Praise Glorious," "Pour on the Power," "Amazing Grace," and "Maybe God Is Tryin' to Tell You Something." The stalwart players captured in this image were teamed as a featured trio. Pictured from left to right are Doug Oravez, Rich Yelinek, and Johnny Glynn.

A crisp visual program, as captured by this snapshot, complimented a solid effort as the Hurricanes continued to thrive in the upper echelon of the DCA in 1992 with a final score of 90.00, notching a fifth-place finish in the championship contest.

"Ben Hur" was the theme for the 1993 and 1994 productions. Mickey Kelly, the show coordinator and color guard instructor, ended his 11-year Hurricanes Hall of Fame career with these Ben Hur shows. Kelly had transformed the fledgling color guard of the late 1970s into a credible unit through his creative flair and trademark intensity. Roman columns enhanced the visual presentation, as shown in this mid-performance photograph from September 4, 1994.

These photographs, taken on August 7, 1993, give a glimpse of the color guard and front ensemble's outfits for the Ben Hur–themed show featured in both 1993 and 1994. These pictures also capture the Hurricanes performing in the pouring rain. Given their time-honored weather-related identity, performing in the rain is something the Hurricanes have never seemed to mind and has most often resulted in spirited performances.

The Hurricanes Hall of Fame was established in 1994 to recognize those individuals who have demonstrated a high level of commitment, dedication, and contribution to the Hurricanes as well as to the marching arts community. As of 2018, the hall of fame has so honored 77 exceptional Hurricanes. There are also 60 Hurricanes of Distinction—individuals who have been recognized through induction into the World Drum Corps Hall of Fame and/or the Drum Corps International Hall of Fame. (Courtesy of the Hurricane archives.)

Shown here is the familiar wedge formation employed for the closing number in 1994 featuring the Hurricanes' theme song from *The Magnificent Seven.* The song was first introduced to the Hurricanes by Joe Genero as a filler song in 1961. It became so popular and so readily identified with the Hurricanes that it has been incorporated into the bylaws, establishing that it will forever be played by the Hurricanes, be it as part of the show, retreat ceremonies, or a parade.

Drum corps is fun and at times can have surprises. This was the case at the DCA Championships on September 4, 1994, when the contrabass line deviated from proper decorum and showed up for retreat ceremonies ready for a toga party! They are shown here backing up Doug Oravez as he belts out his signature "Mag 7" solo. Oravez performed this solo to perfection countless times over his 40-year Hurricanes career.

This group photograph was taken at the DCA Championships in Scranton, Pennsylvania, on September 2, 1995. The Hurricanes celebrated 40 years as a competitive drum corps in 1995 by revisiting a selection of tunes that had been so well received in the past: "Stormy Weather," "Rhapsody in Blue"/Concerto in F, "They Call the Wind Maria," and "The Magnificent Seven" were the vehicles that brought them fifth place in this year, with a score of 90.60.

The Hurricanes are shown entering the field in 1995 before morphing into their opening formation, which mimicked the corps' "Storm Warning" logo shield. The Hurricanes of 1991, 1992, 1993, 1994, and 1995 had indeed re-established the drum corps as a top-echelon DCA contender by placing in the prestigious top five in each of those years.

Long-tenured drill designer Neal Smith returned to pen the drill for the 1995 anniversary year. Smith was noted for his fast-paced designs that effectively integrated the color guard, and he did not disappoint with the 1995 edition. In this photograph from 1995, the color guard frames soloist Clarence "C.J." Johnson.

The 1996 Hurricanes presented a very entertaining show with musical selections from *The Lion King*. The crafty percussion feature pictured above and the elaborate color guard outfits shown below hint at the fun this production entailed. "To Die For," "Hippo Attack," "Bail Out," and "Umulu," as well as a *The Lion King* medley, rounded out the musical selections for 1996. The Hurricanes slipped into ninth place at the DCAs, with a score of 94.00. Lisa Petrucelli is front and center below.

These Hurricanes of 1997 played an enjoyable jazz show, but the quality had once again slipped a tad due to shrinking membership. When the veterans began to trickle out following the 1995 season, their numbers and talent could not easily be replaced. Recruiting efforts geared towards local high school bands was yielding limited results. The image of the Hurricanes as a senior corps was not an easy fit for many high schoolers. The strategy for recruiting was slowly becoming effective but would take time to refine and mature. For these members of the late 1990s, however, the Hurricanes experience was as exciting and rewarding as it has always been.

This 1997 image appears to capture the essence of satisfaction with the group effort and camaraderie as these Hurricanes pose for an impromptu picture following retreat at the last show of the year, the DCA Championship. From left to right are (first row) Scott Friend; (second row) John Curran Jr., Tito Deaz Jr., Tito Deaz Sr., and John Curran Sr.; (third row) Steve Gangi, Sam Descoteaux, Mike Nygaard, Danny Staffieri, Jeff Wasbes, and Jay Reed. (Courtesy of Cheryl Curran.)

New uniforms were once again the big change for 1998, and they arrived just in time for Memorial Day. What a welcome sight to see the Hurricanes decked out in crisp new uniforms, sporting a fresh look of kelly-green jackets adorned by a white citation cord and silver buttons, a black and silver lightning bolt across the chest, white pants and shoes, and the black Hurricane military-style hat topping it off.

The Hurricanes of 1998 played a show presentation comprising jazz and swing with selections of "Baroque Samba," "Stella by Starlight," and "Swing, Swing, Swing." Six trap sets were effectively utilized for a snappy percussion feature, as captured in this image.

Color guard captain Rich Tardie and the American flag honor guard stand at parade rest fronting the Hurricanes in this photograph of retreat ceremonies from the DCA Championships of 1998. They finished the year in seventh position by garnering a final score of 87.70 in championship competition.

The Hurricanes of 1999 enjoyed a wonderful season while playing a show that was not only well-received but was pure Hurricanes in the *Magnificent Seven* Suite from the original sound track. The show proved very popular with drum corps fans, and that always translates to a fun season. With a final score of 90.10, the Hurricanes finished the season in a very satisfying and competitive sixth place in the DCA Championships.

The color guard was a prominent feature of the 1999 production, and they had a blast embracing their role. The choreography and Western-styled outfits the guard donned, replete with bloomers and straw hats, were the perfect complement to this fun and entertaining presentation.

Playing the *Magnificent Seven* Suite was not only a hit with DCA audiences, it also served to inspire excellence from the brass and percussion sections alike. It was truly a fun show to perform. Given the status and tradition "Mag 7" embodies in Hurricane history, the show took on special meaning. The Hurricane horn line looked crisp on the field, above, while the percussion, below, also shined.

Six

Finding the Groove in a New Century 2000–2009

The new century brought with it high expectations. A unique program in 2000 entitled "Celtic Pride" was a compilation of Irish tunes that was widely touted as the most original show of the year. The 2000 Hurricanes progressed much like the 1999 corps, with marked improvement week to week that peeked at the DCAs with sixth place and an impressive 91.30 score.

The year of 2001, however, ushered in a few years of disappointment and adjustment as membership numbers took a slight dip. The image of the Hurricanes as a senior drum and bugle corps was at last identified as a significant detriment to drawing high school–age members. Since its beginning in 1932, when the drum corps was populated largely by World War I veterans, the organization was geared to adults. Although through the decades membership did get younger, the Hurricanes were functioning as an adult organization. When the DCA changed its model from a senior drum corps association to an all-age entity, it became evident, and necessary, to change the culture and perception of the Hurricanes to one that would be welcoming and, most importantly, appropriate for younger members. The culture would undergo immediate adjustments; the perception and realization that the Hurricanes were now a wholesome and largely youth-oriented organization would take a few years to soak in.

By mid-decade, the Hurricanes were flourishing once again. The long-running recruitment dilemma was finally under control, and the Hurricanes would be riding a wave of success through the end of the decade.

"Celtic Pride" was the show theme in 2000, and the Hurricanes looked sharp performing it. The season began with the Hurricanes wearing the traditional hat. It was soon replaced by a shako and tall white plume, giving a more statuesque look that, in combination with the crisp white pants, made for a bright, clean appearance. In the photograph above, the Hurricane horns make a statement en masse in 2000, while the picture below shows the battery looking to be in fine form, also in 2000. The green shako and white plume was a refreshing change that complimented the uniform nicely.

This image captures the 2000 Hurricanes looking smart as they step out on parade. Since 1932, parades have been the cornerstone of the Hurricanes' financial wellbeing. The need to fund operations and maintain equipment is a never-ending responsibility. A busy parade schedule also offers the opportunity for exposure throughout the communities of the region to enhance recruitment, as well as to have a little fun.

The bugles are polished and lined up with the shakos in preparation for a performance in 2001. "Storm Warning" was the chosen show theme for 2001 and featured "You Are My Sunshine," "Stormy Weather," "Come In from the Rain," and "Somewhere over the Rainbow." The quality of the show did not meet expectations, and the Hurricanes slipped to a 10th-place finish at the DCA Championships this year.

Brass instructor and lead drum major Pat Chagnon is shown conducting from the podium in 2001, left, while in the image below, Al DeSantis (on cymbals) and Rich Yelinek (playing a solo) are featured performers during a parade in 2001. They are entertaining a delighted crowd along the parade route with the Hurricanes' official song, a medley of "Hang 'Em High" and "The Magnificent Seven."

Moe Knox, noted drum corps photographer and Hurricane alumnus from the 1950s, is shown in his vintage Hurricane jacket working his table in 2002. In his career of over 50 years, it has been estimated that Knox has snapped in excess of 100,000 photographs of just about every drum corps across America. Pictured below is the 2002 color guard expressing themselves in a photograph taken by none other than Moe Knox. (Right, courtesy of the Hurricane archives.)

In this photograph, Jaime Cutrone, the popular Hurricane drum major of 2002, is shown engaging an audience from the main podium. Her standard answer, when asked by a public address announcer at a competition if the corps was ready to take the field of competition, was a resounding reply: "Yes, we are so ready!"

With the flags unfurled and flying high, color guard captain Rich Tardie leads the American flag honor guard down Capital Avenue in the Great Street Parade of the Barnum Festival in Bridgeport, Connecticut, in July 2003.

With the advent of themed shows came the ever-expanding use of props to enhance the visual appeal of the shows. The above photograph shows the Hurricanes' elaborate effort to capture the feeling of their Las Vegas theme of 2003, while drum major Jaime Cutrone acknowledges an appreciative crowd as she leads a youthful drum line in review in 2003 below. The "Hurcs Take Vegas" show featured such tunes as "Godzilla Eats Las Vegas," "Viva Las Vegas," the theme from *I Dream of Jeannie*, "The Magnificent Seven," "Bacchanal," "I'll Be Seeing You," and "Heartbreak Hotel." In posting a final score of 84.30, the Hurricanes were denied a place in the top 10, placing 11th.

The cake says it all, as there was cause for celebration in 2004. The Hurricanes marked 50 years as a competitive drum corps. Members and alumni came from far and wide to commemorate the occasion at the Hurricanes' annual home show, Fanfare, as well as to attend a large picnic the following day that was sponsored by the alumni association.

Veteran Hurricanes returned in 2004 and were featured in vintage uniforms as the Hurricanes paid tribute to their past. From left to right are Tom Brady, Bob Glovna, Tom Eaton, Art Hlywa, and Jim Nestor. Musical selections that year featured "Rhapsody in Blue," "Make His Praise Glorious," and "The Storm," resulting in a score of 84.475, which was good for a return to the top 10 and ninth place at the DCA Championship competition.

Hurricane members gather around Joe Genero in this photograph as he addresses the corps. He is delivering words of wisdom and encouragement to the membership prior to a performance in August 2004. Genero was actively involved with the Hurricanes in parts of six decades, most notably as the musical director and brass arranger/instructor for 20 years, lead drum major for several seasons, and service on the board of directors. He was also instrumental in the formation of the Hurricanes Alumni Association. He is a Hurricane legend and drum corps icon who inspired excellence and epitomized the phrase "Hurricane for life." Sadly, the Hurricane Hall of Famer and mentor passed a few short months after this picture was taken. (Courtesy of the Hurricane archives.)

These photographs show Hurricanes on parade in 2005. That is Pete Propfe front and center above. The Hurricanes had adopted gold sashes as a tribute to their golden anniversary the previous year. The theme for 2005 was "The Year It All Began" and included the musical selections "The Year It All Began," "Frankie Machine," and "To Kill a Mockingbird." A final score of 84.425 would bring the Hurricanes another 10th-place finish in 2005. In the picture below, the chrome bass drums dazzle in the sunlight.

Pictured at right is contrabass player Teddy Furman. He is shown making a new friend as the corps pauses while on parade in 2005. Was he recruiting? The photograph below captures the color guard leading the Hurricanes as they march in the Barnum Festival's Great Street Parade in Bridgeport, Connecticut, on July 2, 2005.

By 2006, the light at the end of the tunnel was shining brighter and brighter. It seemed as if the long, inhibitive recruiting dilemma had finally been successfully addressed. The high school band competition circuit had gradually gained widespread popularity. The activity, a mirror image of competitive drum corps, consists of field competition and is steeped with drum corps influence. With writing and instruction for high schools, as well as college marching band programs now heavily represented by the drum corps community, the talent pool for the Hurricanes has broadened dramatically. The Hurricanes had taken the necessary steps to harmonize with every faction of the marching arts community. That is Jay Reed anchoring the brass line as they warm up for a performance in this photograph from 2006.

A show featuring the music from *Jesus Christ Superstar* was the Hurricanes' production for 2006. The Hurricanes turned in a respectable finish of seventh place with a score of 88.263 this season. The image above captures a beaming Hurricane color guard, obviously very pleased with their performance; below, the drumline focuses during a feature of the *Jesus Christ Superstar* show of 2006.

The board of directors left no stone unturned and had positioned the organization for a major, all-encompassing upgrade. Acquisitions over the winter of 2006–2007 completely re-outfitted the entire drum corps with new B-flat brass instruments, new drums, new front ensemble equipment, and new uniforms. The excitement throughout the winter, with new equipment coming through the door every week, was unprecedented. The new uniform is a striking, contemporary design featuring a black and white jacket with a folded-down breast panel, accented by a vivid green lightning bolt, black pants and shoes, black gloves and gauntlets with vivid green accents, and the traditional Hurricanes hat. The new equipment, instruments, and uniforms, as well as an exciting show based on the music of Leonard Bernstein, inspired the Hurricanes toward a seventh-place finish with a score of 92.488 at the DCA finals. The new look is on full display in this full corps photograph of the Hurricanes in action at the DCA Championships on September 1, 2007, in Rochester, New York.

The enthusiasm was palpable in 2007, as the long-term forecasts from the "eye of the storm" were encouraging indeed. In this image, discipline and pride seem to radiate as the Hurricanes debut their new uniforms on Memorial Day in North Haven, Connecticut, in 2007.

Drum major Kate Soucha, who led the Hurricanes to a second-place finish in the Barnum Festival's Champions on Parade the previous night, is shown leading the Hurricanes on parade on June 29, 2008, in the festival's Great Street Parade in Bridgeport, Connecticut.

The show theme of 2008 was "Journey West" and featured a selection of Western songs: "Billy the Kid," "They Call the Wind Maria," "Hoedown," and "The Magnificent Seven." These Hurricanes found themselves in the winner's circle three times and ultimately finished fifth in the DCA Championships. The 2008 Hurricanes were led onto the field by color guard captain Rich Tardie and the highly acclaimed American flag honor guard, above, while Lindsey Beaumont of the championship color guard is captured on the lookout and scouting the way for the "Journey West" below.

The Hurricanes capitalized on their successful Western theme of 2008 and went even farther west in 2009, building on the theme with a show titled "The Gold Rush." One of the largest Hurricane corps in recent memory had a fun season in 2009 by notching five trips to the winners' circle as well as contending for the DCA title all the way to the end. The Hurricanes are shown on parade above, with stalwart Thomas Greenhalgh featured playing the solo for the longtime Hurricanes standard "The Magnificent Seven," while below, the battery makes an impressive showing as they pass in review in another image from 2009.

The tuba line is big and bold in 2009, above, while the color guard flashes their brilliance below, as the Hurricanes notched a second consecutive top-five placement with a fourth-place finish and a 95.838 score. The show, themed "The Gold Rush," featured musical selections "Call of the Mountain," "Theme from *Can-Can*," "The Red Pony," "Grover's Corners," and "Silverado." Also noteworthy capping off 2009 was the completion of two well-deserved consecutive undefeated seasons by the color guard, as well as the American flag honor guard garnering their sixth of seven consecutive Best Honor Guard trophies in 2009.

Seven

A Few Bruises but Going Strong in the Teens 2010–2018

Since its inception in 1963, the DCA had indeed matured and thrived. By the time the calendar had flipped to a new century, the DCA had expanded and also witnessed international growth. Originally a Northeastern phenomenon, the circuit now spreads coast to coast and attracts corps from other continents as well. The DCA now represents a broad range of corps from across the country and presents its annual championship each year in what is truly a world championship of drum corps. In any given year, there are now 25 to 30 drum corps competing at the DCA's championship weekend

As of 2010, the Hurricanes were performing well, and there was great enthusiasm surrounding the organization going forwards. They entered the fresh decade having placed in the coveted top five over the past two years. The year 2010 shaped up as expected, and the Hurricanes continued to be highly competitive. The Hurricanes found themselves in the winner's circle numerous times and continued to perform at a high level, flourishing in their top-five status for another three years, through 2012.

In the wake of those five successful top-five years, the Hurricanes' fortunes took a dip. The drum corps became slightly smaller, and some nagging financial concerns also had an effect. The Hurricanes, however, possessing their inherent fire and enthusiasm, produced some very enjoyable shows and continued to have fun despite slipping into the second division of the DCA.

This image from 2010 captures the color guard beautifully framing soloist Tyler Propfe as he plays a passage from the show titled "Heaven Sent," which featured musical selections of "Gloria," "Joyful, Joyful We Adore Thee," "God Said," and "Before the Throne of God Above." (Courtesy of Chris Maher.)

As depicted in this picture from 2010, the Hurricanes' visual program had style as well as precision. In this highly competitive season, the Hurricanes powered to a fourth-place finish at the DCA Championships, with a final score of 95.338. (Courtesy of Chris Maher.)

Drum major Vidal Orduz stands in stark contrast against a night sky as he salutes a chief judge, thus signaling the Hurricanes' readiness to enter the field of competition in 2011. Orduz would lead the Hurricanes to a fourth-place finish in the championships in 2011. (Courtesy of Chris Maher.)

With props in hand, the Hurricanes entered the field in 2011 to deliver a highly entertaining show based on the music of the revered George Gershwin. Gershwin's music is well known and has always lent itself nicely to the drum corps theater, and the Hurricanes have capitalized on the appeal of his music many times over the years.

The 2011 show, titled "Old, New and Blue," was a tribute to George Gershwin, with musical selections *Porgy & Bess*, Concerto in F, "Rhapsody in Blue," "But Not for Me," and "Fascinating Rhythm." Above is a terrific action photograph of Rudy Camacho capturing him in full competitive mode in 2011. The Hurricanes seized upon the emotion of this powerful image and subsequently used it for promotional material. (Courtesy of Lawrence Eckert.)

The brass added an extra layer of dynamics by employing an old-fashion high leg lift to effectively sell a passage of the 2012 production, entitled "Blokes and Birds." It was a lively show blending British pop music from the 1960s with traditional music also of British origin. (Courtesy of Chris Maher.)

The 2012 "Blokes and Birds" program won high acclaim, as it featured musical selections of "Rule Britannia," "Downtown," "Georgy Girl," "Windy," First Suite in E-Flat, "Greensleeves," "Water Music," "Major Modern," "Crown Imperial," "The Windmills of Your Mind," "Fantasia on the Dargason," "Turn, Turn," "God Save the Queen," and *A Young Person's Guide to the Orchestra*. The Hurricanes color guard complimented the theme in British Union Jack replica outfits (above), while percussionist Chris Mauro jams on a trap set (below).

A clever show poster was devised to promote the 2013 Hurricanes. "Rage against the Machine" was the theme chosen for the 2013 production, taking a glimpse to the future as it highlighted such tunes as "Enter the Machine," "The Machine," "Mechanical Love," "Same at the Lake," Revenge of the Fallen," "Flynn Lives," and "My Name Is Lincoln." The drop out of the top five was steep, as the Hurricanes finished in ninth place that year with a disappointing score of 84.85. (Courtesy of the Hurricane archives.)

In this image from 2014, the snare line exhibits expertise and deftness as they execute a high-speed maneuver beautifully. Pictured from left to right are A.J. Frierson, Charles Book, Eric Arsenault, Chris Cossuto, and Ted Lionetti. (Courtesy of Chris Maher.)

In 2015, Rich Yelinec, the talented veteran Hurricane soloist who has delighted drum corps fans for over three decades, dazzles them once again on his "Dizzy Gillespie" horn during the show entitled "After Hours," featuring such tunes as "Sing, Sing, Sing," "Since I Don't Have You," "Nutville," "Harlem Nocturne," and "Jump Jive an' Wail," (Courtesy of Lawrence Eckert.)

The Hurricanes color guard are all smiles as they prepare to enter the competition in Clifton, New Jersey, in 2015. At the head of the line are guard members Lauren Sember (left) and Becca Tobin (right). The smiles displayed by the guard as they are about to enter the field of competition speaks to their confidence. (From the Hurricanes archives.)

In this 2015 picture, the youth of today is shown demonstrating the flair and dexterity necessary to perform the modern-day shows. These well-rehearsed Hurricanes are Katie Garrison (left) and Leah Piros (right). The Hurricanes would place 10th at the DCA Championship contest with a final score of 83.80. (Courtesy of Pat Chagnon.)

In the photograph above, drum major Brian "Soap" Maroldt is shown silhouetted against the night sky in 2016 as he salutes an appreciative audience. Flanking him on the podium is the ever-present symbol of the Hurricanes: the inspirational hurricane warning flags. In 2017 and 2018, Maroldt would depart the podium and serve as the Hurricanes' executive director. (Courtesy of Pat Chagnon.)

The joy of performing and competition, as well as the joy of being a Hurricane, is written all over the face of Briana Lopez as she hits her marks during a performance in 2016, seen at right. One can also appreciate the concentration and focus required to effectively execute as captured in the photograph below of the front ensemble. The 2016 production was titled "Freedom" and presented musical selections of "Amazing Grace," "Freedom," "Nelle Tue Mani," and "Freedom Trilogy." With a score of 82.25, the Hurricanes finished the season in the 13th position at the DCA Championships in 2016. (Both, courtesy of Pat Chagnon.)

Pictured is another useful tool employed to attract new members. Director Brian Maroldt and his team devised comprehensive strategies that had teeth, and the Hurricanes were once again on a positive trajectory in 2017. A fall out of the top 10 notwithstanding, the Hurricanes were growing, healthy, and possessed a palpable sense of confidence moving forwards. (Courtesy of the Hurricane archives.)

This photograph captures the Hurricane drum line performing in 2017. A very entertaining show once again featured the timeless music of George Gershwin's *Porgy & Bess*, including "My Man's Gone Now," "Summertime," "Bess, You Is My Woman Now," "It Ain't Necessarily So," and "Oh, Lord, I'm On My Way" to delighted fans. (Courtesy of Larry Eckert.)

A cluster of baritones pauses to make a statement in 2017. The Hurricanes were once again placed in the 13th position at the DCA Championships, with a score of 79.78, yet the placement did little to dampen the spirit and enthusiasm the Hurricanes were expressing, as they looked ahead with a very healthy and positive outlook. Good things were happening, and they knew it. (Courtesy of Larry Eckert.)

A striking new uniform was unveiled for 2018. It is a contemporary design highlighted by a very prominent field of vivid green lightning striking the right chest, right arm, and right upper leg. It is topped with a black shako and a black plume, also highlighted in vivid green. In this photograph, Vinny and Bella Cataudella are shown attending to details and keeping things orderly as they prepare the uniforms for distribution. (Courtesy of the Hurricane archives.)

These action shots of the Hurricanes in their new uniforms are from a performance on August 18, 2018, in Woodbridge, New Jersey. This performance, viewed in retrospect, was one of the most energetic of the season. Irony is again in full view as the Hurricanes generated this spirited, high-voltage performance in the pouring rain—there is that weather connection again. Anthony Lafond is the drummer front and center on quads in the photograph above, while the photograph below captures the silks looking radiant and seemingly unaffected by the rain. Shown from left to right as they put forth a spirited performance despite the rain are Kristen Hubble and Brittany Boudreau. (Both, courtesy of Chris Maher.)

Pick a caption for the picture above: "Intensity," "Focus," or "Enjoyment." They all apply as any one of these superlatives can be read on the face of Lernard Brand as he bears down during that rain-soaked Woodbridge performance. Below, David Pyrch also demonstrates a tone of concentration as he exhibits fine form in the rain. The rain does not hurt the brass instruments, and it fired up the Hurricanes to excel on this night. It is too bad the remainder of the competition was rained out, but it was a memorable performance none the less. (Both, courtesy of Chris Maher.)

The Hurricanes of 2018 enjoyed a wonderfully rewarding season as they thoroughly embraced their program crafted and based on Greek mythology, titled "Clash Atop Olympus," and navigated the summer schedule on their way to a ninth-place finish in the DCA Championships. The unity, tenacity, and enthusiasm they displayed in 2018 are seen as the catalyst for even better things going forwards, and it appears that the upward trajectory the Hurricanes enjoyed early in the decade has resumed. One thing is certain: these Hurricanes, like all before them, will carry cherished memories and priceless friendships with them for the rest of their lives. As a line of the corps song says, "The Hurricanes, the Hurricanes, walk proud and think of thunder!" (Courtesy of Chris Maher.)

The Hurricanes are eagerly preparing for 2019. The battery is shown above hard at work as they learn a new repertoire, while below, the full ensemble is shown putting their lessons together within the confines of a gym. Earplugs are recommended when the Hurricanes play inside. Winter is, after all, the time of year that produces the foundation for the Hurricanes' prowess. A productive winter typically translates to a fun summer. There is much wisdom in the old saying "Trophies are won when the stadiums are empty." (Both, courtesy of the Hurricane archives.)

A new program was spawned by the Hurricanes in 2017 dubbed the "Brass Choir." It comprises several members of the Hurricane horn line who travel to various locations throughout the community entertaining with Christmas carols and holiday songs. It has become popular and is a wonderful way to create goodwill and spread joy. On that high note, this review of the first 87 years ends. The Hurricanes, originally a neighborhood drum corps, have evolved into a nationally recognized organization. Through 54 years of DCA competition, they have finished in the top ten 49 times and placed in the coveted top five on 24 occasions. Their competitive history has been mercurial at times, and that is okay. Their traditions, popularity, rewarding fellowship, and wholesome spirit have been the guiding light of their longevity and overall success. One would be hard-pressed to find a Hurricanes alum reflecting on their time in the long green line who would not say "I wish I could do it again!" They have touched the hearts of fans and members alike and will continue to do so for years to come, and like the Brass Choir, the Hurricanes spread joy. (Courtesy of the Hurricane archives.)

This final image shows the modern-script logo applique proudly worn on the back of the Hurricanes corps jackets today. Done in green and white, it stands out nicely against the background of their black satin jackets. (Courtesy of Charles King and the Hurricane archives.)

Consistent with our mission to preserve history on a local level, this book was printed in South Carolina on American-made paper and manufactured entirely in the United States. Products carrying the accredited Forest Stewardship Council (FSC) label are printed on 100 percent FSC-certified paper.